Life in the Sea

by Lara Bove

PEARSON

Scott
Foresman

Editorial Offices: Glenview, Illinois • Parsippany, New Jersey • New York, New York
Sales Offices: Needham, Massachusetts • Duluth, Georgia • Glenview, Illinois
Coppell, Texas • Ontario, California • Mesa, Arizona

Opener ©Lawson Wood/Corbis; 1 ©Brandon D. Cole/Corbis; 3 ©Nik Wheeler/Corbis; 4 ©Ric Ergenbright/Corbis; 5 ©Fritz Polking; Frank Lane Picture Agency/Corbis; 7 ©Pat O'Hara/Corbis; 8 ©Ralph A. Clevenger/Corbis; 9 (B) ©Amos Nachoum/Corbis, 9 (Inset)©Brandon D. Cole/Corbis; 10 ©Nik Wheeler/Corbis; 11 ©Lawson Wood/Corbis 13 ©Brandon D. Cole/Corbis; 14 ©David Batterbury; Eye; Ubiquitous/Corbis; 16 ©Royalty-Free/Corbis; 18 ©Robert Yin/Corbis; 20 ©Ralph White/Corbis; 21 ©Al Giddings; 22 ©Jonathan Blair/Corbis

ISBN: 0-328-13578-X

8 9 10 V0G1 14 13 12 11 10 09 08

Beneath the Waves

If you think about the ocean, you might think of boats on the water or **driftwood** dotting the sand. You might imagine someone lying in a **hammock** near the shore or swimming in the surf. But you may not think about all the things that live in the ocean.

More than seventy percent of Earth is covered by water, most of it in the planet's oceans. These oceans are home to thousands upon thousands of life forms. You may think of fish and sharks. Perhaps you have read about sea turtles. But these are just a few of the many creatures found along the ocean shore or beneath the waves.

Waves break against the sandstone cliffs of Cape Kiwanda.

Intertidal Region

The intertidal region is located on the ocean's shores. In this region, the shores get wet during high tide and dry out during low tide. This is why it is called the intertidal region. It is between the tides. This region is divided into four zones: splash, high tide, mid-tide, and low tide. Different creatures live in each zone.

The Splash Zone

Animals and plants that live in the splash zone only get wet from waves splashing on them during high tide. Most of the time this area is dry. Only a few sea creatures live here. Black lichens are plants that live on rocks in the splash zone. In the splash zone you might also see varieties of snails, such as black periwinkles and limpets.

High Tide Zone

The high tide zone is wetter than the splash zone. It gets fully soaked twice a day during high tide, but it still dries up. Sea life in the high tide zone must be able to live out of the water for much of the day.

Crabs can live on dry land for hours. They use their strong claws to hang on to slippery rocks. They also use their claws like **tweezers** to pull food from cracks in the rocks.

Mid-Tide Zone

The mid-tide zone stays wet much longer than the high tide zone. It dries out only during low tide, and it has much more sea life. Here you can see many creatures that usually are found in deeper water. Creatures in this zone have developed ways to stay put when waves crash and stay wet when the tide is out.

One creature that can be seen in this area is the sea anemone. Sea anemones look like flowers but are actually animals. They use poisonous tentacles to paralyze their prey. Once an animal has been paralyzed, the anemone pulls it in and eats it. Sea anemones eat small fish and shrimp. Larger anemones also eat crabs, sea stars, mussels, and limpets. To stay wet during low tide, anemones pull in their tentacles and close up. When they are closed, they blend in well with the rocks.

Sea stars and mussels are found in both the high tide zone and the mid-tide zone. Mussels close their shells tight when the tide goes out. Sea stars are flexible and can cling tightly to rocks using suction. This is especially helpful in the crashing waves of rising and falling tides. Sea stars also use suction to help them eat. A sea star will wrap itself around a mussel and use suction to force the mussel open.

Sea anemones and sea stars cling to the rocks. Notice that the sea anemones that are out of the water have closed up. >

Low Tide Zone

The low tide zone is the wettest in the intertidal region. It never completely dries out. Here you can still see many of the creatures of the mid-tide zone, but you will also find animals from deeper water.

Sea urchins eat seaweed from tide pools that form during high tide. During low tide, they hide in holes in rocks to keep from drying out. The holes also protect them from the force of the pounding waves.

Nudibranchs are often called sea slugs. These brightly colored creatures are in fact slugs—snails without shells. They range in size from microscopic to twelve inches in length, though most are less than three inches long. They can be found in a region that stretches from the low tide zone to hundreds of feet under water. They eat many things, including sponges, coral, anemones, jellyfish, and even other nudibranchs.

A nudibranch

Coral Reefs

Another ocean region is the coral reef. Coral reefs are found in shallow, tropical waters worldwide. Coral needs warm, clear water to grow. Coral reefs are areas of tremendous diversity and abundant sea life. The reefs look like piles of rocks with gardens on top. The gardens are living corals and the rocks are the skeletons of dead corals.

Corals can be pink, green, orange, red, or violet, but most are yellow-brown. Corals get their color from **algae** that live in the coral.

Soft coral with open polyps

< Clusters of grape algae on coral reef

9

Corals are actually tiny animals. The body of the coral animal is called a polyp. The polyp is hollow and shaped like a cylinder. The base of the coral polyp is anchored to rock or to other corals. Tiny tentacles for gathering food surround the mouth of the coral polyp. Because the coral does not move, it relies on water currents to carry food to the waiting tentacles.

Only the stony corals build up the reef. The polyps of stony corals remove calcium carbonate from seawater to build themselves outer skeletons. This is the same mineral that we find in limestone. In fact, limestone comes from ancient coral reefs.

Soft corals are the most brightly colored corals. They grow in colonies that form structures that look like branches, fingers, or shelves.

The Ocean's Rain Forest

Scientists sometimes call coral reefs the ocean's rain forest because they have so many different types of plants and animals for the amount of space they cover. There are more than 2,000 different types of coral, plus there are thousands of other animals, including fish, clams, snails, seastars, worms, eels, turtles, and more.

A coral reef

Among the thousands of fish found on and around the coral reef are scorpion fish, stonefish, lionfish, parrotfish, and barracudas. Most of the fish on the reef are colorful and beautiful. They can be bright yellow, purple, blue, red, turquoise, or silver. The lionfish has dramatic stripes that warn predators away from its poisonous spines.

Some fish don't want to be seen, however. Camouflage helps scorpion fish and stonefish stay **concealed** among the corals. Their colors blend with the color of the sand. These fish can lie unseen on the sand waiting for prey, popping out to capture a passing fish in their large mouths.

The octopus is another creature that uses camouflage to hunt, as well as to stay safe from predators. An octopus can change its color to match its surroundings, blending in with rocks, coral, or sand.

Coral reefs are also homes to mollusks. A mollusk is a sea animal without bones. Mollusks include clams, oysters, snails, nudibranchs, octopuses, and squid.

Can you see the octopus in this section of corals? >

13

Day and Night

Corals behave differently during the day than they do at night. During the day corals retract, protecting themselves from predator fish, which are active during the day. Then, at night, corals stretch out and catch food carried by the water currents.

Danger for Coral

Corals have a delicate layer of mucous that protects them. Mucous gives the coral a slippery exterior that algae have trouble attaching to. Unfortunately, this mucous is easily destroyed by divers. If a diver touches it, the mucous layer breaks down. If the layer is damaged, algae can grow on it and kill the living coral.

Coral reefs can break apart naturally. Reefs break when a section grows too large for the limestone base. Interestingly, nature uses these breaks to help the coral reefs grow. Some of the broken pieces survive and form new coral reefs, allowing reefs to get bigger over time.

< The Great Barrier Reef in Australia is the largest group of coral reefs in the world.

The Sea Floor

The ground beneath the waves is called the sea floor or ocean bed. The sea floor varies dramatically in depth, from shallow waters along the shore to thousands of feet deep. But even in one depth of water, the sea floor varies from one area to another. Just as on land, you can find mud, sand, or rock.

Mud, Sand, or Rock

In shallow waters, clams and sea worms bury themselves in mud or sand, where they can live safely, letting water currents bring them their food. Stingrays and flat fish cover themselves with sand to hide while they wait for prey. They then burst out from under the sand and grab the passing fish.

The stingray gets its name from the sharp spines on the end of its tail, which it will snap upward if a careless swimmer should step on its back. The spines are poisonous, and the wound the swimmer gets will be extremely painful. Lifeguards in warm areas where stingrays live **sternly** warn swimmers to shuffle their feet as they enter the water so that they will scare away stingrays and not step on them.

< A blue spotted stingray on the ocean floor, covering itself with sand

Crabs can walk on top of the mud, bury themselves in the sand, or hide in holes in the rock. Eels also like to live in rock holes, as do octopuses. Both eels and octopuses hide by day in the rocks and come out at night to hunt for food.

Deep Water

As the water gets deeper, there is less light. Go deep enough, and there is no light at all. Creatures become more unusual as the water gets deeper, each adapted to its own environment.

Crinoids look like strange flowers. In fact, crinoids with long stalks look so much like flowers that they are called sea lilies. But crinoids are animals. Some crinoids, called feather starts, live in shallower water, but most crinoids live in deep water.

Crinoids in deep water rely on food that drifts down to them. As small animals die, or as larger animals drop scraps of their own meals, bits of food drift down to the depths. In really deep water, where there is no sunlight and therefore no algae, most creatures rely entirely on this slow shower of food from the upper levels.

< A red crinoid
on coral polyps

Hydrothermal Vents

In 1977 a hydrothermal vent was discovered in one of the deepest parts of the ocean. Many other hydrothermal vents have been found since then, most at a depth of about 7,000 feet.

Hydro means "water," and *thermal* means "heat," so *hydrothermal* means "having to do with hot water." In some places on the ocean floor, water seeps into cracks in the earth's crust, coming into contact with the hot, molten rock underneath. This superheats the water to as much as 750°F. The water pressure is so great at this depth that it keeps the water from boiling. Instead, the water blasts up through other cracks in the sea floor. The water at this depth is almost freezing, so the hot water cools very quickly.

A chimney formed over a hydrothermal vent

In some places, minerals dissolved in the hot water separate out as the water cools. This can form a chimney over a hydrothermal vent.

Scientists were even more amazed to find that there were creatures living around these vents. In total darkness, and with extremes of heat and cold, it didn't seem possible that anything could survive there— but not only do things survive, they're huge. Giant tubeworms are eight feet long. Clams are the size of dinner plates. How do these creatures live? They have bacteria living inside that produce food for them through *chemosynthesis*, which is like photosynthesis, except it uses chemicals in the water instead of sunlight.

Giant tubeworms live around hydrothermal vents.

21

Research in the Deep Sea

Only in the last thirty years has technology advanced enough to make deep sea research possible. Hydrothermal vents are so far below the surface that researchers have a difficult time conducting research. Using a mini-submarine, two or three people can descend about 8,000 feet. (A scuba diver can descend only about 100 feet.) They collect samples from the vents in special titanium containers that won't melt in the extremely hot water.

Research Continues

Though scientists have **lamented** not making more progress, they have learned much about the oceans' regions and sea life. Already they have learned that there is much more life in the sea than there is on land. Perhaps you can become an oceanographer and continue their important research.

Glossary

algae *n.* plant or plantlike organisms that live in oceans, lakes, rivers, or ponds; a single organism is called an alga

concealed *v.* hidden

driftwood *n.* wood floating in the water

hammock *n.* swinging bed made of fabric

lamented *v.* regretted or wished that something had not happened

sea urchins *n.* small, round, soft-bodied sea creatures with spiny shells

sternly *adv.* in a very strict or serious way

tweezers *n.* tools used to pick up small items